www.SFNonfictionBooks.com

MEET THE SHARKS

Dive into a World of Adventure!

Welcome to the thrilling underwater realm of sharks! This isn't just any coloring book; it's a journey filled with action, fun, and learning. As you color your way through these pages, you'll also discover amazing and safe facts about these magnificent creatures.

From the majestic Great White to the elusive Hammerhead, every page brings a new adventure and a new shark to learn about. But that's not all! Engaging activities await to challenge your mind and enhance the fun. So grab your favorite coloring tools, and let's embark on an oceanic adventure together!

THE AMAZING GREAT WHITE SHARK

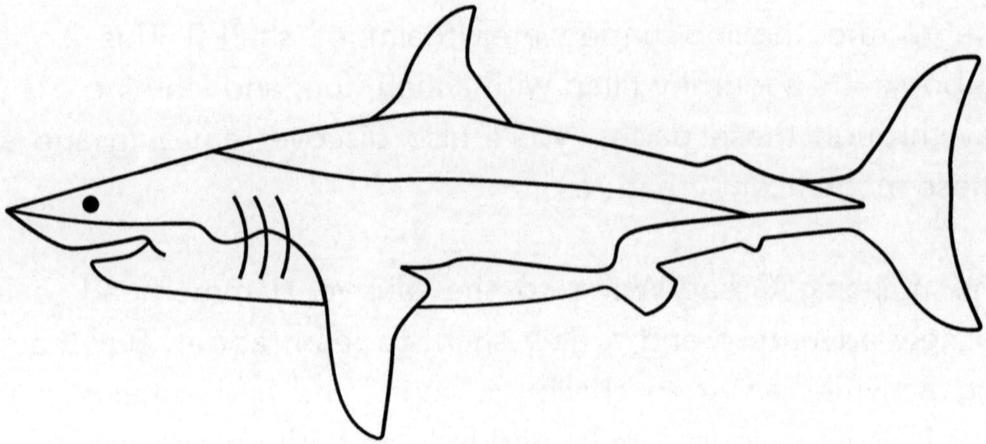

Hey everyone! I'm Gary the Great White Shark!

Many know me as "The Star of the Ocean".

I may have an intimidating appearance, but despite my many teeth I am actually much friendlier than it appears!

DID YOU KNOW?

The Great White Shark has over 300 serrated teeth arranged in multiple rows!

The Great White Shark has a Torpedo-shaped body that allows them to easily hunt prey, such as one of their favorites - seals.

THE STRIPED STAR - TIGER SHARK

Hello there! My name is Tina the Striped Star. Commonly known as a Tiger Shark.

My unique stripes help make me stand out at ocean parties!

May stripes are dark in the wild, but you can color them anything you want!

DID YOU KNOW?

The Tiger Shark can be identified by the dark and vertical stripes on its body; these markings are particularly seen among younger sharks.

The Tiger Shark has earned its nickname of the "Garbage Can of the Sea", because of its wide-ranging diet. Unfortunately, due to human pollution, they are often found to have eaten non-edible human objects.

THE MIGHTY BULL SHARK

Hello there! My name is Benny the Bull Shark.

Some say I am tough - which is true! What's even cooler is I can swim in both saltwater and freshwater environments - pretty neat right?

DID YOU KNOW?

The Bull Shark has a strong aggressive nature with a large body with a pointed snout.

The Bull Shark is known for its unique ability to live in different water environments.

TRAVELER - OCEANIC WHITETIP SHARK

Aloha! My name is Oliver the Ocean Traveler!

As an Oceanic Whitetip Shark, I enjoy exploring the vast ocean waters by waving my white-tipped fins.

Join me on an adventure together!

DID YOU KNOW?

The Ocean Whitetip Shark spends much of its time in large seas, far from shores, and often follows pilot fish.

The Oceanic Whitetip Shark is an aquatic long-distance traveler and is known for being super curious

THE SPEEDY SHORTFIN MAKO SHARK

Zoom! Did you see that?

That was me, Max the Speedy Shortfin Mako Shark. I'm one of the fastest fish in the sea!

Are you up for a race?

DID YOU KNOW?

The Shortfin Mako Shark is widely recognized as one of the fastest species of shark, reaching speeds up to 45 mph!

They have a sleek body, a beautiful metallic blue hue and short sharp teeth.

THE UNUSUAL HAMMERHEAD SHARK

I'm Hannah, the Unusual Hammerhead Shark.

With my wide, flat head and distinctive features, my unique appearance helps me better locate snacks in the sand.

DID YOU KNOW?

Hammerhead Sharks have a wide head that helps improve their vision and can reach 20 feet long.

The Hammerhead Shark derives its name from its distinctive, hammer-shaped head which it uses to enhance its senses and find food hidden beneath the sand.

THE BRIGHT LEMON SHARK

My name is Lucy, the Bright Lemon Shark.

With my cheerful yellow skin, I bring some brightness into the deep blue sea!

Come join my crew and help spread some cheer!

DID YOU KNOW?

Lemon sharks are friendly. You can often see them out hanging with each other.

Lemon sharks usually live in shallow waters with sandy bottoms, where they can reach 11 feet long

THE MYSTERIOUS BLUE SHARK

Welcome from the deep blue sea! I am Blu, the Mysterious Blue Shark.

With my deep blue color and love of exploration, I enjoy diving deep into the ocean's mysteries to unveil its secrets!

Want to come on an ocean quest with me?

DID YOU KNOW?

Blue Sharks are known for producing large litters; in some instances, mothers can birth as many as 100 babies at one time!

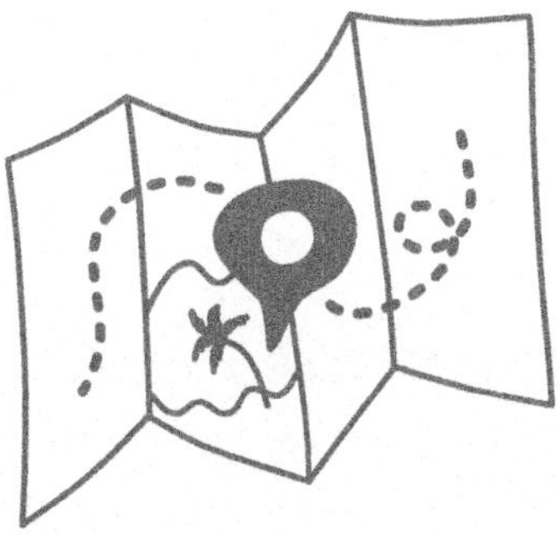

Blue Sharks prefer cooler waters to swim in and love to travel long distances

THE SPOTTED SAND TIGER SHARK

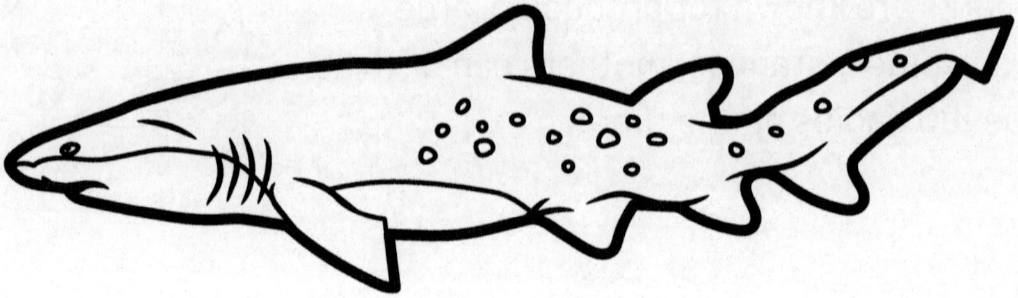

Hey there! My name is Sammy the Spotted Sand Tiger Shark, also known as a Grey Nurse Shark.

While my spots might resemble a starlit galaxy, they help me blend with the ocean floor.

DID YOU KNOW?

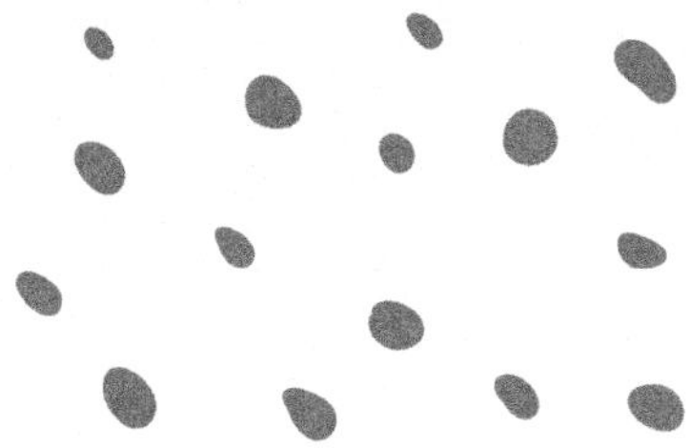

The Sand Tiger Shark stands out with its distinct reddish-brown spots on its body and can grow up to 10.5 feet long

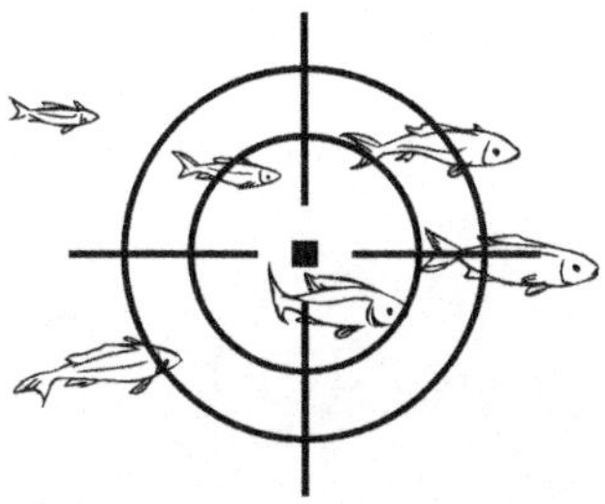

Unlike most shark species, they float instead of submerging themselves beneath the water, giving them an advantage when hunting prey in shallower waters.

THE AGILE BLACKTIP SHARK

What's up, friends? My name is Andy the Agile Blacktip Shark.

Take a look at my cool black-tipped fins! I enjoy doing flips and twirls in the water; why don't you join in the fun?"

DID YOU KNOW?

Blacktip Sharks are highly agile swimmers and are known for breaching (leaping out of the water to hunt schools of fish).

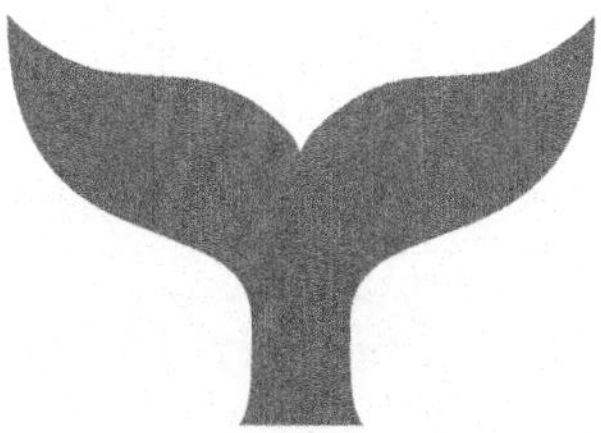

The Blacktip Shark derives its name from its distinctive black fin tips. Relative to other shark species, they tend to be smaller - growing only up to five feet long.

TRUE OR FALSE?

Read the questions carefully and choose the best answer for each.
Color the shark blue if it's true, and red if it's not.

	TRUE	FALSE
The Bull Shark has a wide and flat head.		
The Great White Shark has 300 pointed teeth		
The Spotted Sand Tiger Shark loves to swim in deep waters		
Lemon Sharks are friendly and joins there friends for a swim		
The Shortfin Mako Shark is the fastest shark of all		

LIFE CYCLE OF SHARKS

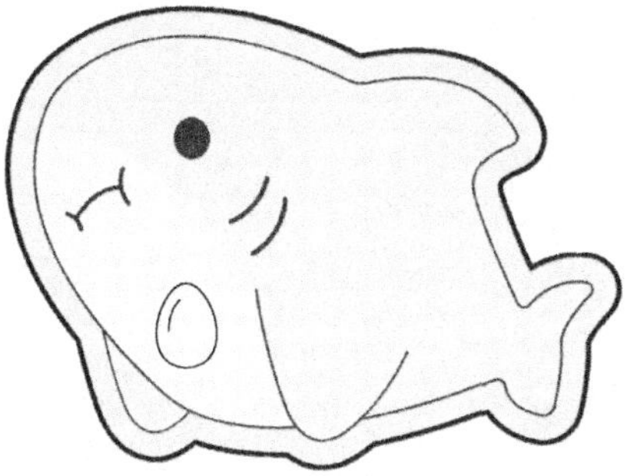

Oviparity

Some sharks lay eggs in a special case to keep them safe (Oviparity).

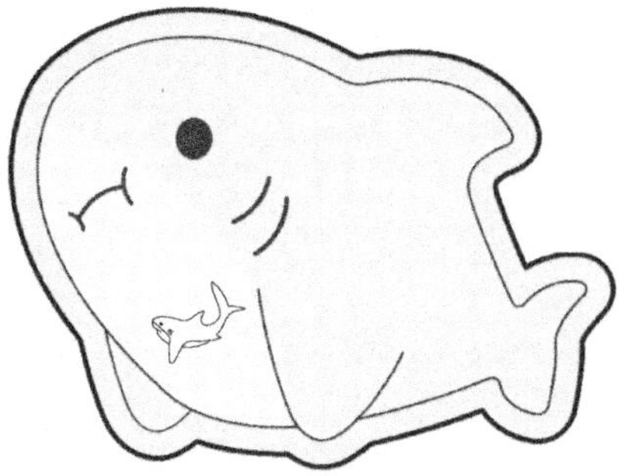

Ovoviviparity

Other sharks have baby sharks hatch inside them and then give birth (Ovoviviparity).

Sometimes, the first baby shark to hatch might eat the other eggs inside.

LIFE CYCLE OF SHARKS

Pup Stage

Once a shark has been born or hatched, it is known as a pup. Pups typically come out with fully developed teeth ready to take on life on their own right away.

LIFE CYCLE OF SHARKS

Juvenile Stage

As baby sharks grow bigger, they become 'young sharks' or 'juveniles'. They learn important things like how to hunt.

These young sharks aren't ready to have their own babies yet.

LIFE CYCLE OF SHARKS

Adult Stage

When sharks are all grown up, they become adults. Adult sharks find partners and can have babies, either by laying eggs or giving birth.

Some sharks can live a very long time, even longer than many pet dogs!

Sharky's Life Cycle Quest

Draw the journey of a shark on your page, starting from a pregnant shark, then a baby shark, growing into a playful young one, and finally becoming a big, strong adult shark!

PARTS OF THE SHARK

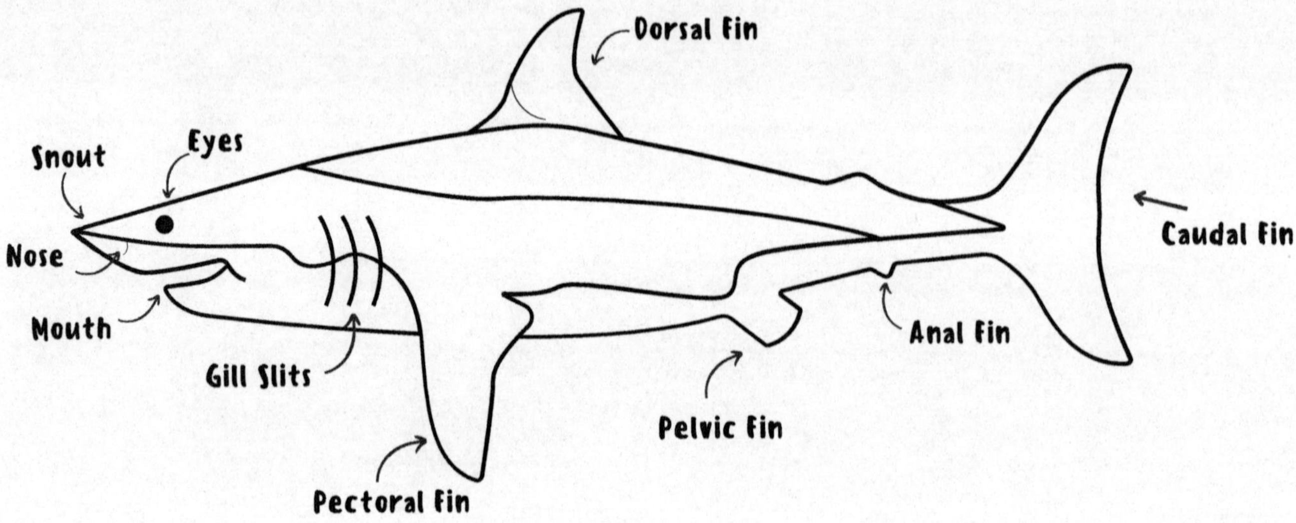

SHARK ANATOMY

Eyes: Like you, sharks use their eyes to observe everything that's going on around them. Some shark species even protect their eyes with special covers so they won't get hurt while munching away at food!

Nose: Sharks have an amazing nose. They don't use it to breathe, but instead, they use it to smell and find their food. Imagine being able to smell your favorite snack from hundreds of meters away!

Snout: A shark's snout is the pointy part of its face that sticks out in front. It helps to poke around and feel for things in front of it.

Mouth: Here comes the exciting (or scary...) part! Sharks boast large mouths filled with hundreds of sharp teeth. These sharp teeth allow sharks to catch, grip, slice and munch their food easily!

Gill Slits: You know how you breathe with your lungs? Well sharks, like all fish, use gill to breathe. They take in water through their mouth, and then the water goes out through the gill slits, giving them oxygen. These slits look like little lines on the sides of their head.

SHARK FINS

Dorsal Fin: The fin on the back. It helps the shark stay straight and not tip over.

Pectoral Fins: The fins on the sides near the head. They help the shark turn left and right.

Pelvic Fins: These fins are a bit further back on the sides, near the belly. They help the shark balance.

Anal Fin: The fin on the bottom, near the tail. It helps the shark stay steady.

Caudal Fin: The shark's tail. It pushes the shark forward, like how we use our legs to walk.

FINTASTIC SHARK ADVENTURE!

Can you name Sharky's special fins and parts?

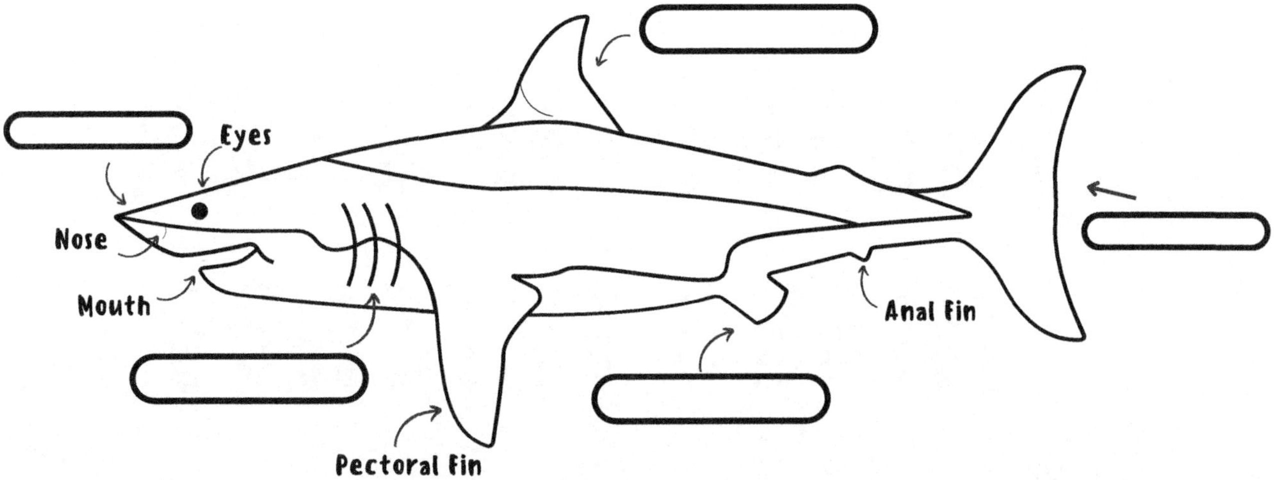

Have fun coloring him in too!

PROTECTING OUR SHARK FRIENDS

SHARKS ARE LIKE OCEAN DOCTORS!

Just like doctors keep us healthy, sharks keep the ocean healthy. They help balance the number of other fish and creatures, so everyone gets a fair share of food. When sharks are around, the oceans are happy and well!

SHARKS MAKE SURE EVERYONE GETS A TURN!

Sharks make sure not one kind of fish takes all of the available resources. By doing so, they ensure that there are enough plants and creatures in the water for everyone!

SHARKS HELP OUR OCEANS STAY CLEAN!

By eating weak or sick fish, sharks help keep the fish populations strong and healthy. It's like they're the ocean's cleanup crew!

BUT SHARKS ARE IN TROUBLE...

Too Much Fishing: Some people fish way too many sharks for their fins or meat, which is unhealthy. We must be careful not to take more sharks than the ocean can replace.

Lost Homes: Sharks require a healthy ocean to exist in the same way as birds require trees. However, humans occasionally throw trash into the water or destroy areas where sharks like to hang out.

Not-So-Nice Nets: Sharks can become trapped in large nets by mistake. Because sharks cannot swim free, these nets can be dangerous.

I AM TRAPPED! HELP ME!

The shark got trapped along the way and needs your help! Draw a path out of this maze and help him swim away to his friends. Don' let him near orcas nor dolphins!

START HERE

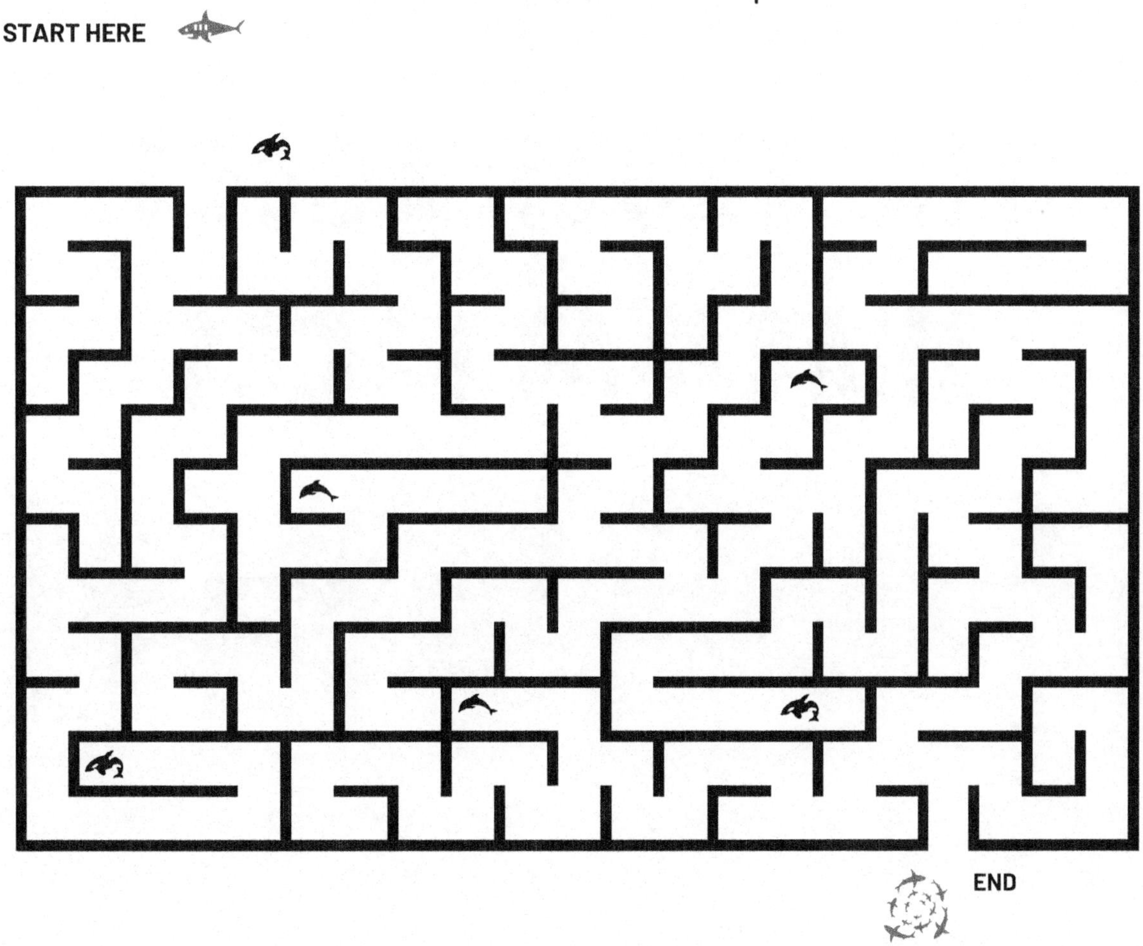

END

THE TRUTH ABOUT SHARK ATTACKS

FACTS ABOUT SHARKS

Sharks are Curious Creatures!

Sometimes sharks may bump into people because they're curious and want to know what's going on; much like when we touch something new for the first time and see how it feels!

Oops! Mistaken Identity!

Sharks sometimes attack when they mistake a human being for a seal or fish. Because they don't use glasses, these sharks can make mistakes that lead them to bite someone by mistake!

Sharks Don't Really Like How We Taste

Sharks usually prefer eating fish or seals, and will generally relax once they realize a person isn't their target snack. We aren't on their menu!

FACTS ABOUT SHARKS

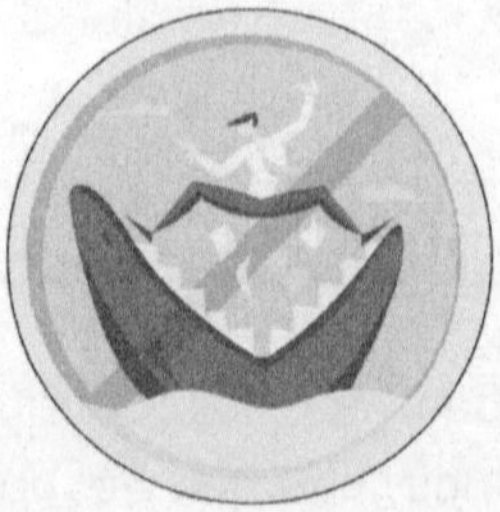

Shark Attacks are Super Rare

You're more likely to be struck by lightning you than being attacked by a shark. Shark attacks are very, very rare!

Sharks Are More Scared of Us!

Most sharks swim away when they see humans; they tend to be more scared of us than we are of them!

Home Sweet Ocean

Sharks are most comfortable in their own ocean homes, far away from where people like to swim. So, you can keep enjoying the beach - you probably won't come face-to-face with one there!

SHARKS ARE ENDANGERED

Imagine your favorite toy box slowly losing toys because everyone keeps taking them and not putting them back. Soon, there might be no toys left! Similarly, sharks in the ocean are being taken away and not many are left.

We need to help protect them. What do you think you could do to help save the sharks?

SHARK MYTH BUSTED!

Hey there, young ocean explorer! Are you ready to dive deep into the world of sharks and become a **Shark Myth Buster?**

INSTRUCTIONS:

Read the statement on each page and make a guess if it's a fact or fiction. Once you have your answer, shout it out loud! Whether you got it right or not, you're becoming a Shark Myth Buster and that's Jawsome!

QUESTION # 1

Sharks really love eating people.

IS IT FACT OR FICTION?

QUESTION # 2

Movies always tell the true story about sharks.

IS IT FACT OR FICTION?

QUESTION # 3

Sharks love to swim near the beach.

IS IT FACT OR FICTION?

QUESTION # 4

Sharks love to eat fishes

IS IT FACT OR FICTION?

QUESTION # 5

Sharks are scared of people.

IS IT FACT OR FICTION?

SHARK QUIZ

NAME THAT SHARK!

Look at the picture of the shark and guess its name.
Write it in the empty space and have fun coloring the shark.

L_M_ _ S_A_K

NAME THAT SHARK!

Look at the picture of the shark and guess its name.
Write it in the empty space and have fun coloring the shark.

B__L__ __H__R__

NAME THAT SHARK!

Look at the picture of the shark and guess its name.
Write it in the empty space and have fun coloring the shark.

B_U_ S_A_K

NAME THAT SHARK!

Look at the picture of the shark and guess its name.
Write it in the empty space and have fun coloring the shark.

G__E__T W__I__E __H__R__

NAME THAT SHARK!

Look at the picture of the shark and guess its name.
Write it in the empty space and have fun coloring the shark.

M_K_   _H_R_

BE A SHARK HERO!

Our shark friends need a helping hand and YOU have some fantastic ideas! Write down your ideas for saving sharks or draw whatever you like!

i-SPY with my little eye

Ahoy, ocean explorers! Can you find all the hidden sharks? They're really good at hide and seek!

A Sharky Shadow Game!

Match the shark shapes to their shadowy silhouettes and see how many you get right!

- Mako shark
- Great White shark
- Hammerhead shark
- Lemon shark

Rainbow Shark Splash

Color in the shark by matching the numbers to the colors of the rainbow and see your rainbow shark come to life!

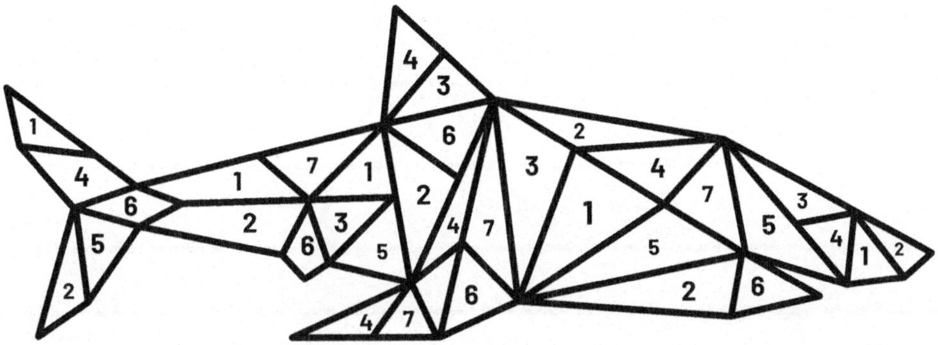

COLOR GUIDE

1 RED

2 ORANGE

3 YELLOW

4 GREEN

5 BLUE

6 INDIGO

7 VIOLET

OCEAN JOURNAL

Hey little explorer! How did those sharks make you feel? Write down your feelings and any fun facts you discovered!

SHARK GLOSSARY

Shark: A big fish that's been around for millions of years. They come in various sizes!

Ocean: A huge body of saltwater where many sharks live.

Migrate: When sharks travel long distances in the ocean.

Prey: The food sharks eat. Some sharks love to munch on seals!

Endangered: Not many of one type of shark left. We should protect them!

Pilot Fish: Small fish that often swim with sharks. They're buddies!!

SHARK GLOSSARY

Traveler: Some sharks move to many places in the ocean.

Shallow Waters: Parts of the ocean that aren't very deep.

Shark Litters: When a momma shark has more than one baby at a time.

Agile Swimmer: A shark that can turn and move very quickly.

Egg Case: Some sharks lay eggs, and babies grow inside. This is called Oviparity.

Ovoviviparity: Some sharks carry eggs inside them, and the babies come out live.

SHARK GLOSSARY

Pup: A baby shark. So cute!

Juvenile Stage: The time when a shark is like a teenager, not a baby but not grown up.

Adult Stage: When a shark is fully grown up.

Fishing Nets: Big nets that people use to catch fish, but sometimes sharks get caught by accident.

Pollution: Bad stuff in the water that can hurt sharks and their homes.

Vision: How sharks see. Some have really good vision in the dark.

SHARK GLOSSARY

Nose: Sharks have a great sense of smell. They can sniff out their food from far away.

Snout: The front part of a shark's head. It's kind of like their nose and forehead combined.

Mouth: This is where sharks munch on their food. Watch out for those teeth.

Dorsal Fin: The fin on top! It helps the shark balance and steer. You might see this one sticking out of the water.

SHARK GLOSSARY

Pectoral Fin: The side fins that look like wings. They help sharks swim straight and turn.

Pelvic Fin: Fins on the shark's bottom half. They help with turning and stopping.

Anal Fin: A fin near the shark's tail. It's another helper for balance.

Caudal Fin: The tail fin! This one gives sharks speed and power to zoom through the ocean.

OCEAN EXPLORER

This identification card certifies

____

has succeeded in solving the mysteries surrounding shark species, behaviors, and habitats by traveling to the ocean's depths.

DATE

CONTINUE THE CREATIVE JOURNEY!

This shark adventure is just a glimpse! Dive into a whole collection of coloring and activity books that spark imagination and curiosity in every child. See more now.

ABOUT THE AUTHOR

Aventuras has three passions: travel, writing, and learning new skills.

Combining these three things, Miss Viaje spends her time exploring the world and learning about anything and everything that interests her, from yoga, to music, to science, and more.

Aventuras takes what she discovers and shares it through her books.

www.SFNonfictionBooks.com

Printed in Great Britain
by Amazon

50633359R00040